I Lived What You Said

LARRY COLEMAN

LegitHouse Publishing
Edmond, Oklahoma

I Lived What You Said
Larry Coleman
Copyright © 2025 by Larry Coleman
Published by LegitHouse Publishing
ISBN: 979-8-218-64362-1

All rights reserved. No part of this publication may be reproduced, stored or transmitted in any form or by any means, electronic, mechanical, photocopying, recording, scanning, or otherwise without written permission from the publisher. It is illegal to copy this book, post it to a website, or distribute it by any other means without permission.

First edition

Cover art by Larry Coleman
Art and Quotes by Larry Coleman
Photography by Hana' Sahar Photography

UNIT ONE
- W.O.R.L.D.
- UNDERSTANDING
- BALANCE
- BIRTH
- WHO GONE LOVE THE BABY
- BEFORE YOU START
- QUIET NOISE
- DIET AND EXERCISE
- CONVERT-SATION
- TIZZY
- ANGER
- H.A.I.R.
- ANGRY
- OUTDONE

UNIT TWO
- TRADITION
- MAN OF GOD
- CHURCH FOLK
- EMBRACING THE SETBACK
- THE BELIEVER
- SON OF MAN
- ALL ON YOU
- OWN IT
- CONSIDERATION
- WISDOM
- GROW
- OWNERSHIP
- MISTAKES
- THE INSIGHT
- WHAT I LEARNED ABOUT FORGIVENESS
- IF I DID
- MY APOLOGY
- BETTER THAN ME

UNIT THREE
- VISION
- PERCEPTION
- SOCIAL STATUS
- MY VIEW
- THE BOSS
- SPITE
- THE LITTLE THINGS
- THINKING RICH
- FAST
- DO SOMETHING
- MORE
- THE KEYS TO SUCCESS
- UNDERSTANDING

UNIT FOUR
- LOSS
- RULE: 2737
- DEPRESSION
- ABUSE
- 1-35 AND DYING
- ICU
- ACCEPTANCE
- GETTING OFF ENDED
- HITTING HOME
- AND A CHILD SHALL LEAD
- I PRAY YOU NEVER KNOW
- WE ALL HAVE TO CRY
- JOY COMES IN THE MOURNING
- THE GREATEST AMONG YOU
- P.S.
- VOCABULARY WORDS
- ABOUT THE AUTHOR

DEDICATION

In a heartfelt tribute to God's guidance and in loving memory of my mother, this book unfolds the chapters of a life lived true to the values and lessons instilled. May these words serve as a testament to the journey shaped by faith, family, and the enduring spirit of resilience.

~Letha Henrietta Coleman~
1935-1985

ACKNOWLEDGEMENTS

First and foremost, I would like to express my deepest gratitude to my family. Your unwavering support, love, and encouragement have been the foundation upon which this book was built. To my wife Ruby, my daughter Hana', my sons Laterrious and Deon, and my big brother John, thank you for your patience, understanding, and belief in me during this journey. Without your constant inspiration, this book would not have been possible. Every page reflects the strength and love that I've drawn from you all.

With all my love and appreciation, thank you.

UNIT ONE

W.O.R.L.D.

Waking up daily is more than just the traditional sleep and wake routine; it's about observing, understanding opportunities, and taking on responsibilities.
After recognizing my surroundings and opportunities, I ensure they're safe. I reflect and rebound, opening my mind to the reality of the opportunities that come with waking up. Once I've done these things, I can relax in my environment.

Now, an important aspect is the 'L' – I'm Larry, and we all know what 'EL' means. After the initial steps, to have 'L' (meaning 'Live'), I must first have peace, harmony, love, laughter, and the ability to let go. This is essential for living a long life. My goal is to leave a lasting legacy of love, laughter, and longevity – my legacy. I woke up to it, took the opportunity, realized it, and
ran with it. Now, I live it out daily, doing everything I am designed to do because I know it is my destiny and desire to live a divinely ordered life.

This is my 'World.'

Feel free to adjust as needed to suit your personal style better.

UNDERSTANDING

"Too young to understand and too hurt to know better!"
~Larry Coleman

LET'S TALK ABOUT IT

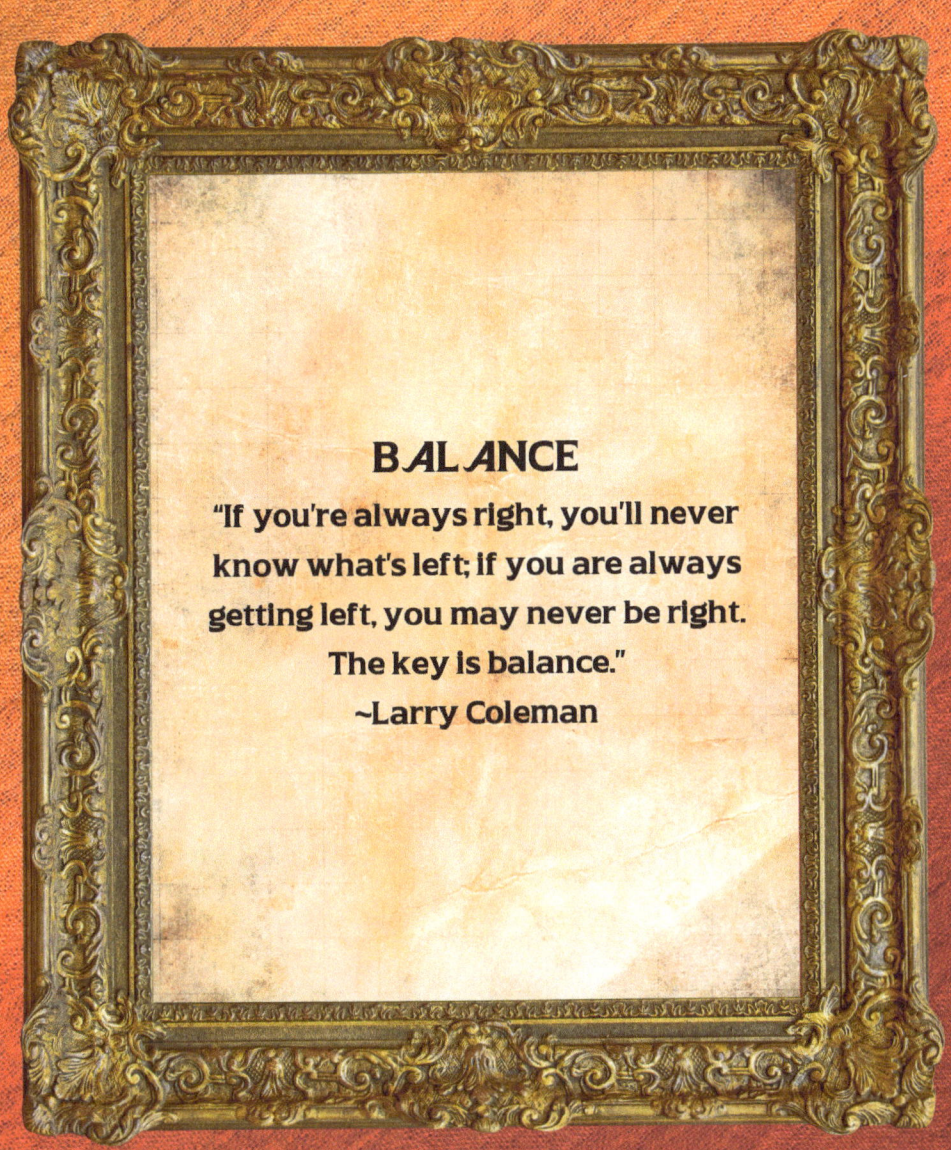

BALANCE

"If you're always right, you'll never know what's left; if you are always getting left, you may never be right. The key is balance."
~Larry Coleman

"BIRTH"

I hung around my daddy his whole life, but we didn't know each other; we never talked. Then he let me go in 1972, then I met my mother, but I never saw her. I stayed with her for nine months, and then she put me out in 1972. I know it sounds ridiculous, but life got better for me. I met them both again in 1972; that's when I finally saw both of their beautiful faces and heard their beautiful voices. I had a whole family of brothers and sisters this entire time! I thought I was alone. God is Good.

~Larry Coleman

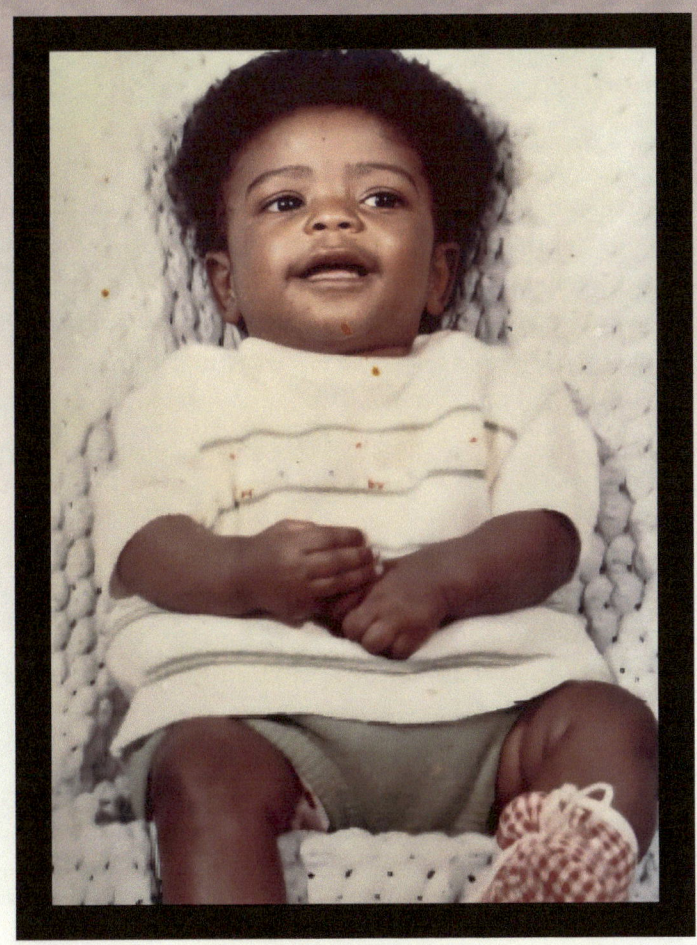

Who Gone Love The Baby?

WHO'S GONE LOVE THE BABY?

Who's gone love baby enough to bypass all the bullshit that has gone on between two individuals in a relationship? After the love is gone, what happens to the baby? Everyone gets caught up in their emotions falls out, and once the smoke clears, the baby is left scared from all the fighting and chaos. But I ask, who's going to love the baby? That's why I choose to love the baby over all the bullshit because no one cares enough to come back into the burning building to save the baby. I love the baby enough to sacrifice my hurt feelings, pride, and hatred for someone else who has pissed me off more than once. Even the offender gets grace for bullshit, but as soon as the shit hits the fan, the baby is the first to be forgotten and not given a second thought. We get locked up in our emotions and leave the baby alone. So, I ask again, who's going to love the baby? I do. I will always choose the baby over some sick, selfish, and hateful adults any day.

LOVE BEYOND THE FLAMES

As the flames of turmoil engulfed the once vibrant love between two individuals, the question echoed through my mind: who would love the baby enough to rise above the tangled mess of emotions? Beyond the chaos and after love's departure, the baby's fate hung in the balance.

After heated arguments and emotional fallout, the baby silently witnessed the strife. Scars of the conflicts lingered, etched on the innocent soul. Yet, amid this wreckage, I was compelled to choose love for the baby over the sea of adult troubles.

The burning building of resentment and pride became a test of my commitment. Few dared to return for the baby amidst the lingering smoke, but I was different.

My love for the baby surpassed personal grievances, hurt feelings, and the darkness of hatred. Even those who caused the turmoil received undeserved grace, yet the baby, the silent victim, often faced neglect.

Locked in the clutches of our emotions, we forgot the one who needed love the most—the baby. In this chapter of life, I declared my allegiance to the innocent, vowing to prioritize the child's well-being over the sick, selfish, and hateful actions of adults. Always, without hesitation, I would choose to love the baby beyond the flames of adversity.

Take care of the baby that you want to be loved! That hurting feeling deep inside you, longing for someone or something to come along and tend to that pain. News Flash! When it comes to your spiritual rescue, you have to be willing to be the hero in your own life to save your baby! Take care of the vehicle of your peace of mind! "The Baby"

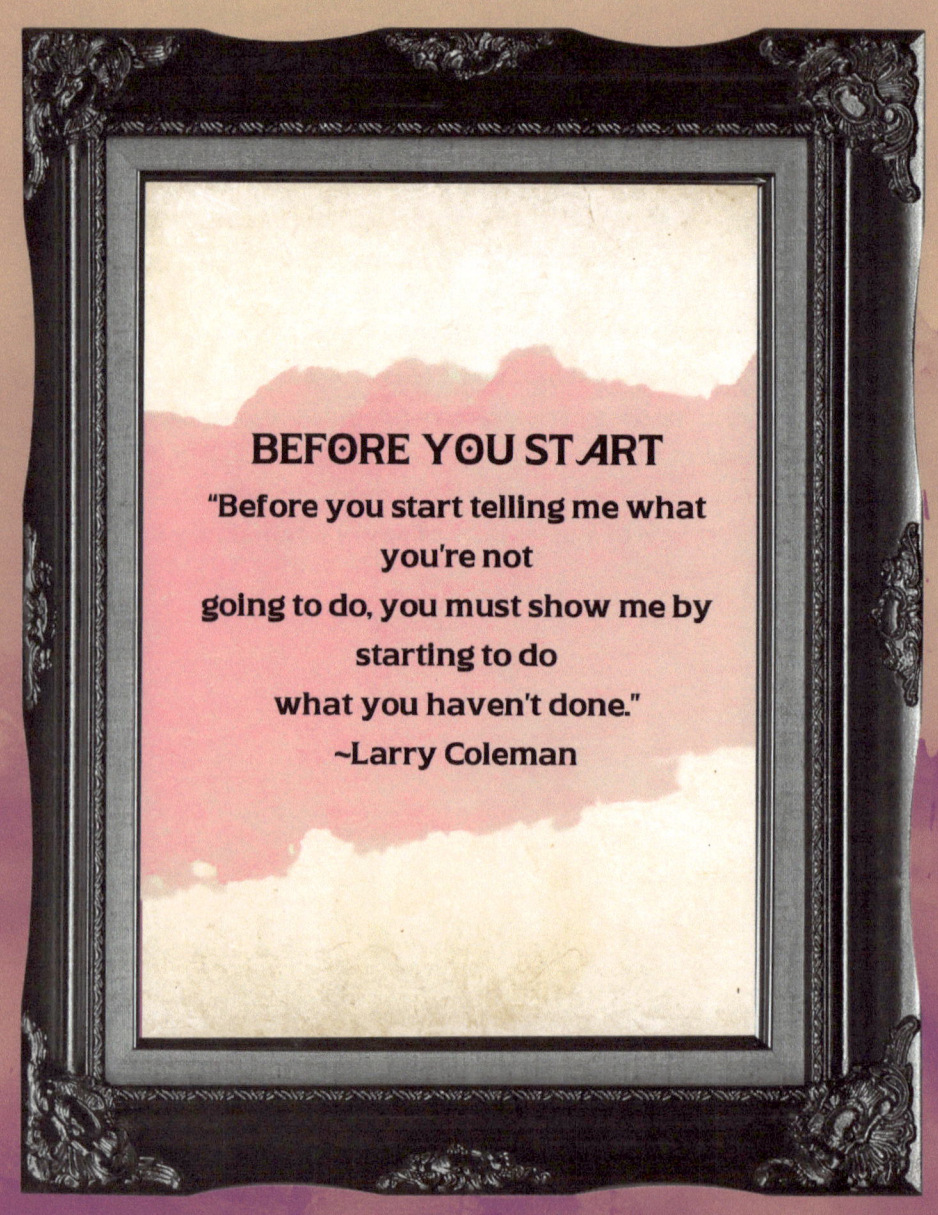

BEFORE YOU START
"Before you start telling me what you're not
going to do, you must show me by starting to do
what you haven't done."
~Larry Coleman

QUIET NOISE

I just now realized why and how I understand why I can sleep through loud noises, why I like to wind down to a movie with the TV kind of loud, and why I can sleep with the lights on or the temperature too cold or too hot. It's simply because, while growing up, I had to learn how to find my peace in the middle of chaos. I don't know if I was good at drowning out or drowning in the noise. We often find comfort in not dealing with our problems amid the noise, but for me, the noise is silence in my mind, genuinely ambient background music setting the scene for peace and understanding the mess that I'm in at the moment.

The brain is a beautiful machine. It allows you to escape the pressure of trauma by locking up memories and storing them deep within the subconscious, protecting you from pain and harmful experiences. When you need to recall those memories, sometimes it may take a miracle to unlock that vault because the brain remembers the body's response to that moment in time. It may not allow you to explore that feeling ever again, or it may replay that memory repeatedly, altering our perception of our reality.

I wish I knew the secrets of controlling brain function when it comes to emotional trauma. I would heal the world of so much pain, but since I don't, I must do my job to help people understand the contribution of emotions and unlock trauma by drowning out the noise through simple peace with positive and negative energy. Both energies are needed to correct the effects of an emotional blast. In my opinion, negative energy is more powerful and beneficial than positive energy when appropriately used to balance the mind in a chaotic episode. Negative energy fuels the courage and power of the mind and body to move in the direction of balance. However, when used only as fuel, it is volatile. It can burn out positive energy, which is the best energy for comprehension and articulation of emotions to settle family matters in a proper balance.

Please understand that the balance of energy is vital to resolve. Too much positive is not valid, and too much negative is not balanced. If you're always right, you'll never know what's left, and if you're always getting left, you may never be right.

DIET AND EXERCISE

Diet and exercise go hand in hand.

Exercise stimulates the mind and thought processes, fostering the discipline to modify your diet. This, in turn, constitutes what we refer to as exercise—putting plans into action for your mind, etc.

Motivation to exercise arises from utilizing your gifts and propelling positive changes in your life. Lift weights to remove obstacles from your mind, body, and soul. Run to expel pain from your body and life.

Stay active, initiate your diet, and embrace exercise!

The process of lifting weight is understanding what your limits are, how you will work out to get out of a current situation you're in if it is out of shape or in shape, learning the shapeshift by diet and exercise to get out of the hell that will cause you to die. That is where I lead to understanding the word press, which is the exercise standard, especially weightlifting.

Press: Any exercise that helps increase muscle strength.

(Keep pressing when times get tough you will get stronger eventually.)

Compress: Pressing something into a smaller space or putting pressure on it from different sides until it gets smaller. Also, compression helps with faster recovery.

(When we feel the pressure of the world causing us to feel smaller, know you'll recover sooner than later and feel much better.)

Suppress: keep secret, redact, or prevent development.

(Exercise can reduce hunger, which helps with weight loss and helps to lighten your load.)

Depress: exercising will help reduce anxiety symptoms.

(So get up and exercise. Don't let anxiety get to you.)

Oppress: Prolonged cruel or unjust treatment or control mental pressure or distress.

(When we are in bad shape and want to create the same shape for others, I call this the dying exercise.)

Impress: Make someone feel admiration and respect—the act of making a mark on an object.

(When we diet and exercise right. We see and feel better about our results. We want to show off for others and make a mark on the world with this positive energy, which is how it should be.)

So we gonna go to the gym and learn how to workout this mental body!

Let's get to the gym and knockout
5 laps of hello how are you
10 I love you sprints
10 reps of apologies
20 reps of forgiveness lifts
 And do a cool down of have a nice day and I love you's!

This will help you burn a lot of stress and lose weight.
You will look fabulous in no time.

CONVERT-SATION

"This is a conversation, not a Convert-sation"
~Larry Coleman

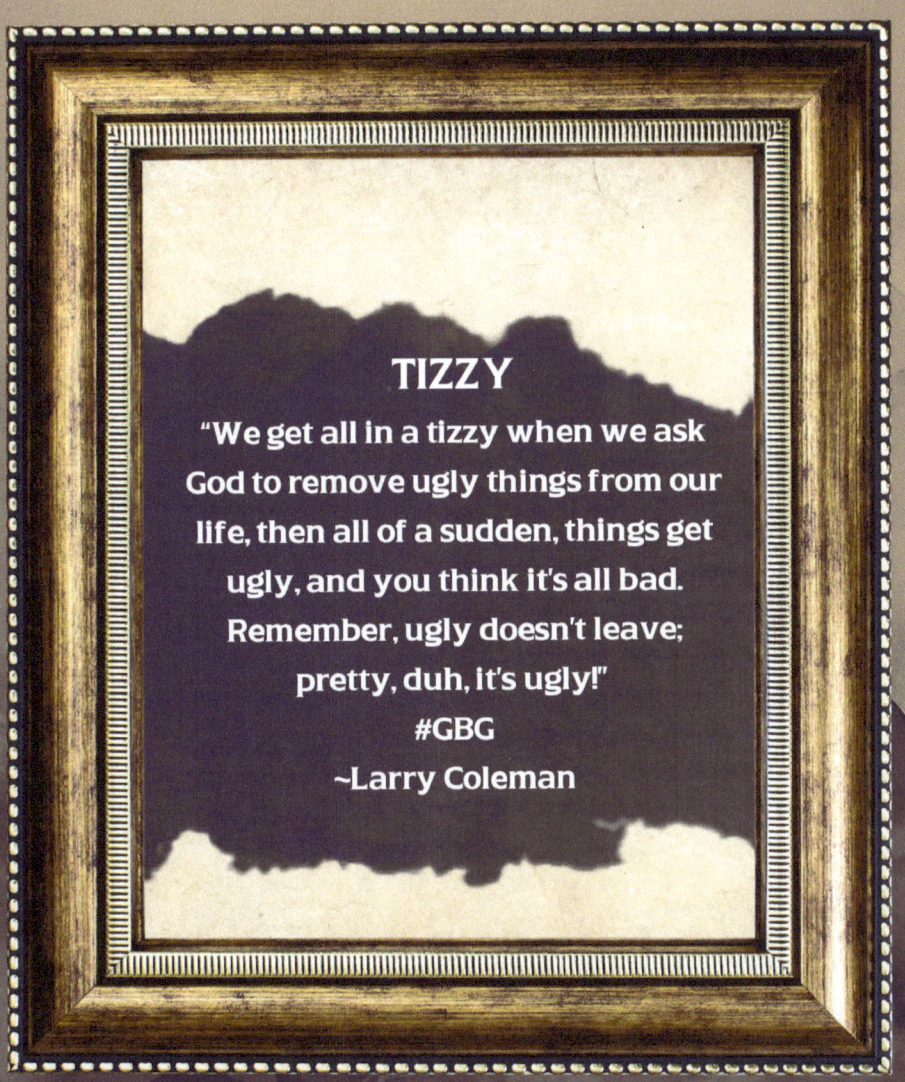

TIZZY

"We get all in a tizzy when we ask God to remove ugly things from our life, then all of a sudden, things get ugly, and you think it's all bad. Remember, ugly doesn't leave; pretty, duh, it's ugly!"
#GBG
~Larry Coleman

ANGER

"Make your Anger so expensive that no one can afford it and your kindness so cheap almost anyone can get it for free."
~Unknown

H.A.I.R.

Having Africans in rows...

Having Aboriginal in rows...

Hatefully Acting in rage...

Didn't like it then, and I don't like it now.

I heard about places like this where boys were bought in places where wars were fought!!

You need control ain't like y'all ain't been doing it the whole time controlling people's hair.. y'all need to control people it's what y'all do.

Having Africans in rows...

Having Aboriginals in rows...

Having Africans and Indians rivaling.

Didn't like it then, and I don't like it now, trying to control my hair.

Didn't like it then and don't like it now. I heard about places where little boys and girls were bought in places where wars were fought you've won more battles, giving success two more rows, showing the world how all investments revealed the real evil intent to keep controlling Hair...didn't like it then and I don't like it now!

-Larry Coleman

ANGRY

A nigga get ready, yea!!

I said AYE! nigga guns rifles yesterday.

Get ready. The war has started!

What if you find yourself in a deep ditch with that same nigga? You got beef with guns to yo head, but you act like ain't seen shit!

AYE! nigga get ready, yea! AYE! nigga get ready yesterday!!

I ask you again, what if you find yourself in a deep ditch with the same niggas you've had beef with? Cops got guns to yo head, but you act like you ain't see shit; get angry about that!!

While Y'all are up here marching and protesting me and my guys are up late night practicing killing with No resting!!

We are up early in the morning, heading to Ferguson, challenging a gang of murderers !!

NOW! Let's see if you Angry enough!!!!

- Larry Coleman

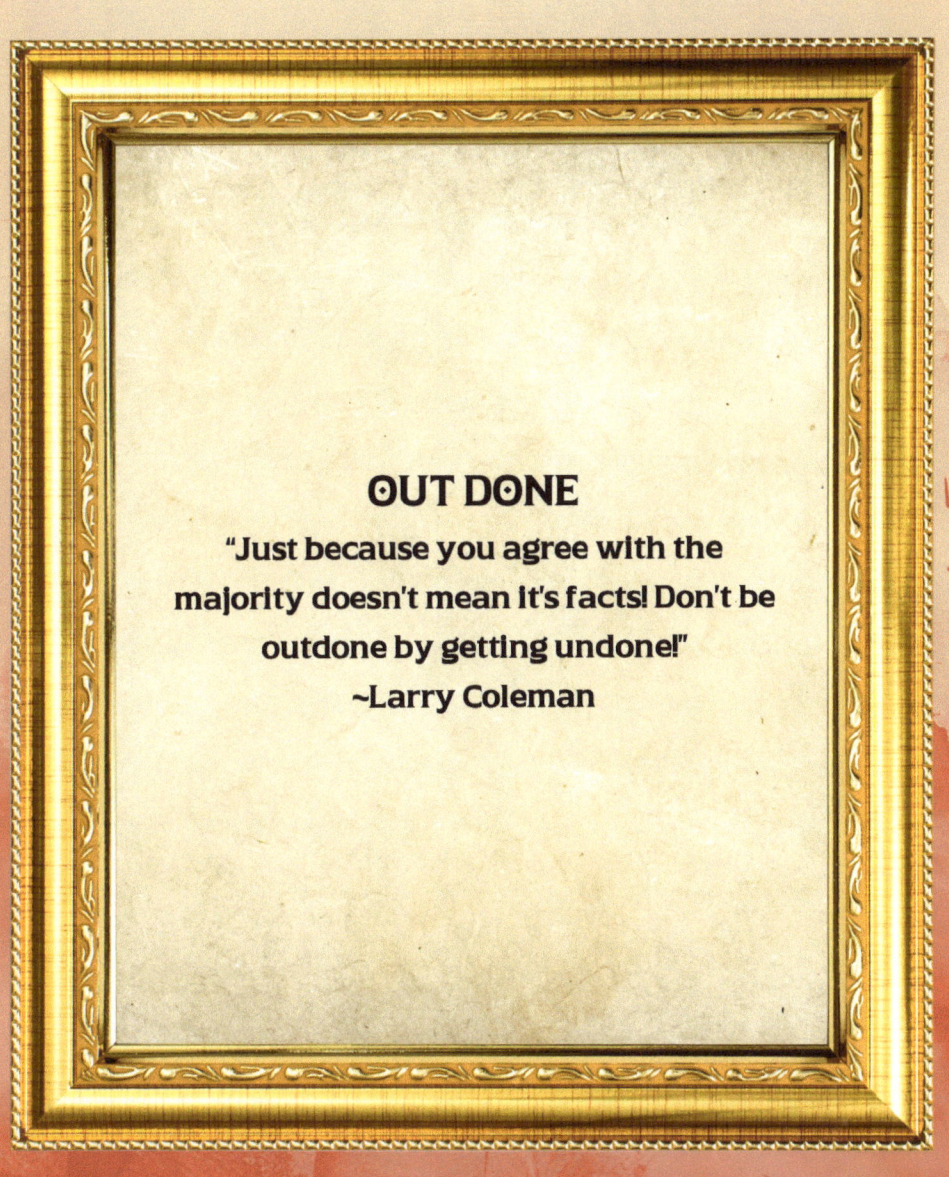

OUT DONE

"Just because you agree with the majority doesn't mean it's facts! Don't be outdone by getting undone!"
~Larry Coleman

UNIT TWO

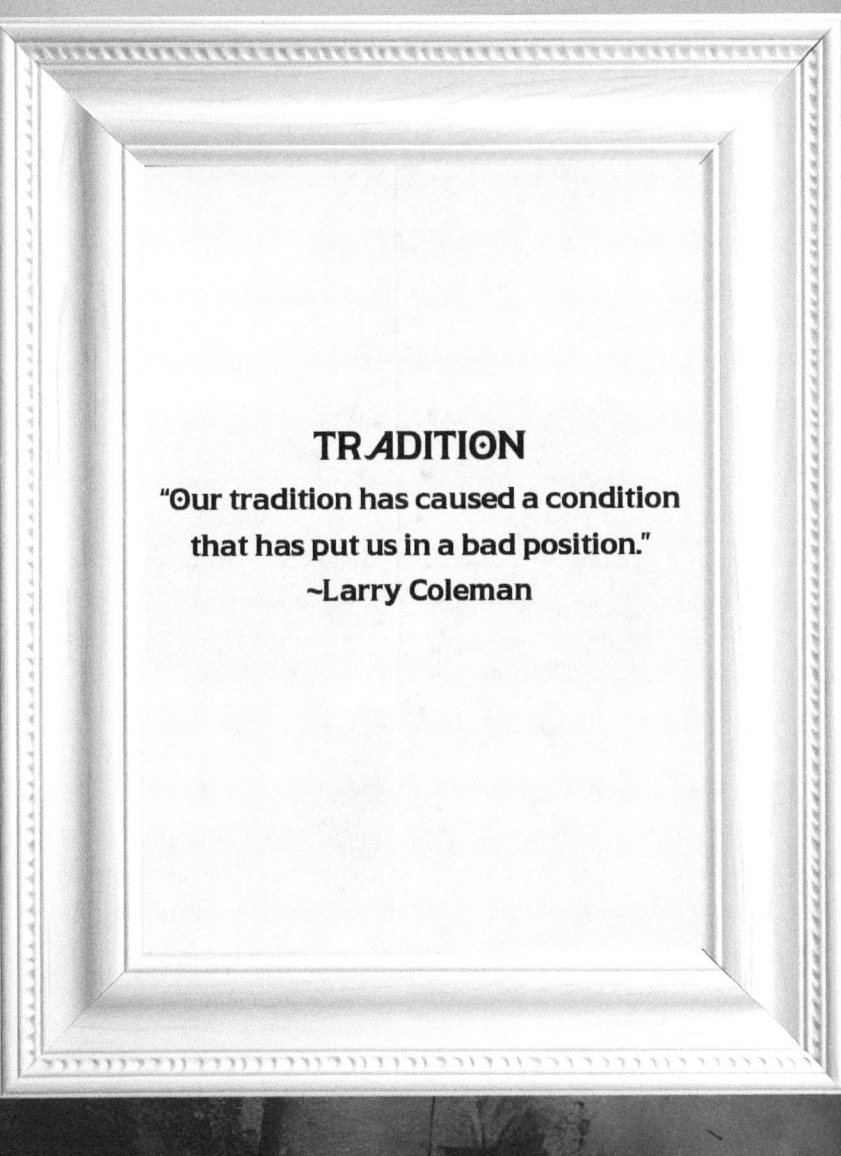

TRADITION

"Our tradition has caused a condition that has put us in a bad position."
~Larry Coleman

MAN OF GOD

As a man of God, I aim to exemplify what God reveals through His word. As a man, I aim to mirror the principles in the world. My godliness should reflect through me. Be mindful that I am like a mirror, and what you present in it will reflect on you. If you are full of hatred and ill will, adjust your view or clean your mirror so you don't cast a bigger projection of your negativity. 'Be as you desire to be done for you'—do unto others as you would have them do unto you.

Look at life, especially your spiritual life, as you would a sport. It's akin to supporting your favorite team in football, basketball, or baseball. We've created cultural lifestyles around celebrating these sports, congregating in large numbers for games, showing support for our players, wearing team apparel, and investing in attending games and autograph sessions. We watch news reports about our players and enjoy highlight reels. Even during losses, we remain loyal fans, supporting them through ups and downs. Now, apply this passion to your spiritual journey, treating it like a sport. Live your life as if you're on the road to the playoffs and, eventually, the championship round. Support your spiritual living, even without commentary and highlight reels. Study and enjoy the 'practice' as if it were a game. Remember that just like great athletes practice without us seeing, we can still see the results in their performance during the game. Stay fit and get in shape to play a hard-fought game in your spiritual life.

CHURCH FOLK

Church folks, man, I can't stand y'all. However, I've been too busy judging people myself. Honestly, I used to think I couldn't stand church folks, and I didn't believe in this god theory. I'm just being honest, y'all. I don't believe in religion at all, and the whole "God won't put anything on you that you can't bear" - pss, whatever!

But, honestly, I noticed I got tired of watching messy church folks misinterpret their Bible teachings, similar to preachers. Then it dawned on me that I wasn't reading my Bible either; I was too busy reading people. That's when I started to learn for myself and gain a fundamental understanding of a good message. Please don't get too excited because I still don't believe everything in this book. It upsets me to see my fellow man/sister being foolish and buying into nonsense like religion and the Bible, making them judgmental and messy.

If it leads you to be a good, caring, and fair person, then I'm all for your path. However, if it destroys your common sense and decent moral character, then poof, be gone with that mess around me.

EMBRACING THE SETBACK

Some people never get the opportunity to sit and relax after a hard day's work, not truly in a sense! We work long hours for years, trying to provide for our families and loved ones. By the time we look up, we realize we've missed many important moments in the lives of our loved ones, especially our children. Only then do we recognize that we've neglected the most crucial person in the whole equation—ourselves.

Our health and peace of mind often take a back seat until a significant life-changing event occurs, knocking us on our butt or, worse, without a chance to grasp the purpose of the dream. So when I say, "Be glad you get to sit down so you can sit back," it's simply a moment of gratitude that, instead of being taken out, we've been sat down, given an opportunity to reflect on what's most important in our lives. Whether it's due to COVID, quarantine, time in the hospital, or being off work due to injury, you can use that time to build on it rather than having your time taken away. So, enjoy the sit-down!

-Larry Coleman

THE BELIEVER

This message is for the believer, the one who desires to follow God and the word of God. It is for those who claim to believe in a most high God who has sent his word to guide humanity in understanding how to live according to his rules. Whether you call it God-like or any other term, it is all per the will of our God.

In today's world, with numerous religions and diverse beliefs about God, this belief system has led to significant division. Sadly, this division has caused us to harbor hatred for our fellow brothers and sisters, all in the name of God. The problem lies in making God's word and will our own belief, not adhering to what the word says but rather following what we feel, driven by a desire to be like God.

Regardless of your beliefs, I want to emphasize that I care about how you are living. As a Be Liver, I will never depart from the will and presence of God. I reiterate I will not be leaving the presence or will of God because I am committed to living my life under God's will for all of humanity.

"True Believer" - Larry Coleman

In the journey of faith and belief, I invite the reader to delve deeper into the concept of living in God's will. It is addressed to the believers—those with a genuine desire to follow God and adhere to His word.

In a world marked by diverse religions and various interpretations of God, the chapter reflects on the unfortunate division caused by differing beliefs. The central message emphasizes that this division often leads to animosity among people who, paradoxically, claim to follow the same divine principles.

The crux lies in individuals making God's word and conforming to their personal beliefs rather than aligning with the actual teachings. The desire to be God-like, to shape God's will according to personal feelings, has resulted in a distorted understanding of spirituality.

The chapter introduces the term "Be Liver," representing an unwavering commitment to living by the will and presence of God. The author, Larry Coleman, states: "I will not be leaving the presence or will of God." This proclamation serves as a foundation for the "True Believer" who is dedicated to living life in alignment with God's will for the betterment of humanity.

As the narrative unfolds, the chapter encourages readers to reflect on their own beliefs and challenges them to prioritize the essence of "Be Living" over doctrinal differences. It aims to foster a sense of unity among believers and emphasizes the importance of embodying the true spirit of faith in daily life. "Be living" serves as a call to live authentically in God's will, transcending divisive beliefs and fostering a genuine connection with the divine.

SON OF MAN

I'll mix the fire with devotions soothe the ocean with the potion of lyrical lotion see I'm a miracle quoting through flowing, blow down the walls of unjust in one thrust, it's a must that I bust this bubble of trouble we called lust what is it that makes of mind Click travel through this thick jungle I wonder why we won't humble ourselves amidst the depths of hell in which we dwell fused in a gel of hatred, materialistically taken out of proportion, put in distorting information to pimp a nation in a compilation of complicating conversation conviscating our minds like a concentration camp bout to sour our souls like damp clothes Lord knows we ain't ready for burdens to heavy that's why we must keep it steady on the straight and narrow keep our eyes on the sparrow, not the duck chicken nor geese, but refrain from the beast especially ones that make yeast 'cause we cease to exist in the presence of God, losing our essence to squabs and jobs all type of distractions detaching us from that everlasting arm it ain't gone be no more leaning, because it's seeming that I let too many demons in my semen got me scheming creaming thru dreaming. I'm even Feenin', like Jodeci. It's hard for you to notice me. I'm not shining like the king that I'm supposed to be.

"If each one would teach one, I am the son of man, they would understand God got the plan." If each one would teach one."

Lord why you fill me with this villainess blood because you knew that I'd be living with thugs giving me drugs that's how I knew your grace was amazing and you kept me in tune to your station steady waking me up out this jungle, but I wonder. if I had a chance to dance in a better land would I be a better man ,but my eclectic mind can't accept it. I'm in a transition mind slipping like a transmission I'm a man wishing I can excel in this spiritual classroom.

Trying to get a curb with my last tune embezzling own fate, scaling my gone weight, but That's a long wait for the wrong date got my cells blocked like cholesterol bout to take out the best of y'all my biggest adversaries are these enzymes in my capillaries breaking me down flynotes that I quote compound like zygotes got me backed up against the wall like spackling messing up textures in my lectures I'm making desperate measures just to be in God's presence, and all I want to do is feel his essence .

"If each one would teach one I am the son of man they would understand God got the plan "if each one would teach one"

Its true I am the son of man, but I am the Spirit of God and if you'll be on my squad, we can wage JIHAD on those at odds with God, because the plan was to make you understand. I'm only man.

"If each one would teach one I am the son of man they would understand God got the plan"if each one would teach one"

ALL ON YOU
"It's all about how you do things or view things.
It's still all on you!"
~Larry Coleman

ALL ON YOU

I plan to change how we see things, especially my definition of things. I'm okay with redefining everything that doesn't line up with my beliefs. I take the opposite meaning or direction. I'm not locked in on right or wrong, left or right, good or bad, or good and evil.

I'm more focused on the direction I'm going. So if your path takes you right and it causes you Hell, then go the opposite direction; just turn around. I dared to change the definition; for example, evil is live turned around! The Devil is lived. So you mean to tell me I'm the devil if I've lived my life? I'm evil if I live? Really? God turned around is Dog, and we call a female Dog a Bitch, so that, in my definition means we got God backward! Ijs Damn, man! Wake up! People.

I'll end with this. The Son (Sun) died for your sin so that you might live! Well, let's turn it around. At the end of a Great Holy month of worship, service, fasting, communal gathering, and spiritual development, it is called Eid to commemorate the Holy Month, where, in my opinion, life is even more apparent in focus. Eid turned around is Die! In some beliefs, they say life starts when you die. In my view, it's all the same with different directions taken.

OWN IT

"Own it, understand it, and fix it! Recognize that it's a generational curse, and the key is to understand that everyone has to play their part. Someone started this problem, and it's persisting, affecting both me and the younger generations. If I identify the issue, it's my responsibility to own it, comprehend it, and address it!"

- **UNVEILING ROOTS**

As I go deeper into the intricacies of the generational curse, I began to unravel the hidden roots that had woven their tendrils through time. Each revelation was a step closer to understanding the origins of the problem that persisted in my family and, by extension, affected the younger generations.

The journey to confront this legacy required a keen awareness of the patterns and behaviors handed down. It became evident that someone in the past had sown the seeds of this challenge, and those seeds had sprouted into a complex web of issues impacting not only me but also the innocence of the children and the generations yet to come.

In this chapter, I embark on a quest to trace the footsteps of those who paved the way for this generational struggle. Every piece of the puzzle I uncover brings me closer to a solution. It's a process of self-discovery, a commitment to owning the past, understanding its intricacies, and, ultimately, setting the stage for transformation.

As I navigate through the corridors of family history, I realize the profound truth that breaking free from the chains of a generational curse requires not only individual responsibility but a collective effort. It calls for everyone to recognize their role in the narrative and actively contribute to the healing process.

Join me as I peel back the layers of time, seeking insights that will empower me to dismantle the inherited challenges and pave the way for a brighter, unburdened future.

CONSIDERATION

Your full-course meal exceeds my ration. Being sick for you is comparable to my own illness. Milk in your eyes stings worse than the acid in mine; your week off work for partying contrasts with my two months off and a week in the hospital post-major surgery. While you enjoy a break, I navigate rent, mortgage bills, and more during my time away from work. Your unpaid bill during leisure time contrasts with mine, accrued due to necessary absence. This isn't a comparison of pain; it's about perspective and personal value. I won't judge but advocate for consideration. Take care of yourself; it's all about perspective and consideration—just consider my ration.

•PERSPECTIVES UNVEILED
In the realm of contrasting experiences, the chapter opens with a nuanced comparison of sickness, where the author vividly depicts the differing intensities between their ailments.

A striking metaphor emerges as the author describes the burning sensation of milk in the eyes, drawing a poignant parallel to the acid in their own eyes. This metaphorical exploration adds layers to the narrative, emphasizing the subjective nature of pain.

The consideration progresses to explore the divergent paths of time off work. While one character revels in a brief respite for partying, the other grapples with an extended absence, navigating financial responsibilities amidst health challenges. The stark contrast highlights the multifaceted nature of individual struggles.

Financial burdens take center stage as the narrative unfolds, with one character juggling rent, mortgage bills, and more during their hiatus. This starkly contrasts with the leisurely break of the other, raising questions about responsibility and priorities.

The tension peaks when an unpaid bill becomes a point of contention, underscoring the consequences of choices made during periods of reprieve. The chapter concludes with a reflection on the central theme—consideration. It serves as a reminder that, regardless of the situation, understanding and empathy should guide actions.

Consideration serves as a pivotal point in the narrative, unraveling the intricacies of contrasting lives and emphasizing the importance of considering others' perspectives. The reader is left contemplating the broader implications of choices and the delicate balance between personal value and collective understanding.

WISDOM

"Wisdom is not merely gained knowledge; rather, it is knowledge applied. Be mindful and pay close attention to how mirrors work - they reflect all things, revealing the opposite of what is in view or displayed. For instance, we often hold onto beliefs from society or past masters without questioning the meaning in the mirror. 'GOD in the mirror is simply a DOG' - a pet we feed, experience joy with, and sometimes hurt, only for it to bite us in response. Yet, we often fail to understand that it's just a dog, no less."

THE REFLECTIVE JOURNEY
As we look into the essence of wisdom, we uncover the profound concept that wisdom transcends mere knowledge acquisition; it is a force awakened when knowledge is applied with discernment.

In this chapter, let us focus on the metaphor of mirrors, urging us to be vigilant and attentive to their workings. Mirrors, the silent observers of our existence, reflect not only what is presented before them but also unveil the concealed truths. They reveal opposites, prompting us to question the beliefs instilled by society and past masters.

Consider the mirror a reflective entity, challenging the unquestioned acceptance of teachings. "GOD in the mirror is simply a DOG" becomes a thought-provoking analogy. Like a pet, our wisdom may bring joy, but it can also bite back when misunderstood or mistreated. It is a reminder that our knowledge is, in essence, a companion—a dynamic force that responds to our actions.

I want us to embrace the reflective journey to explore the meanings within the mirrors of our lives. As we unravel the layers of perception, we uncover the transformative power of applied knowledge, leading us further along the path of true wisdom.

GROW

"We want to grow in the change, but won't change to grow!"
~ Larry Coleman

GROW

The process of forgiving involves letting go of what you dislike about a person and focusing on the positive aspects. This becomes simpler when relying on old memories to shape new ones, allowing for a fresh start without dwelling on past offenses. It is commonly stated that overcoming deep emotional wounds is challenging, yet achieving true peace requires active effort and kindness. Reminiscing about past offenses contradicts the pursuit of peace, emphasizing the need to cultivate a peaceful mindset.

I've often heard someone say they ain't gone change! The only thing they will change is their hair color, which will be one color. I believe that is an unfortunate and lonely mentality, especially when the change needed to be made is from mean to kind. It's funny we say we don't want to change, but we constantly try to force others around us to change. For example, imagine having a child who's battling drug abuse and is struggling to get off of drugs and is in and out of prison simply because they can't seem to change their ways. You have tried everything in your power to get them to change for the better, but at the same time, you're not willing to change your mean behavior, not even your hair color!!

Wow, now let me ask you this: if you believe in the power of Change, and you really want to help someone to better their lives, and the only thing that would help is change ... would you do it? Sometimes, we want to grow in the change but won't change to grow.

LET'S TALK ABOUT IT

OWNERSHIP

We have grown accustomed to embracing lies and getting offended by the truth. We must break these cycles on a personal level. It's common to feel anger when a loved one points out the truth about us, yet we readily embrace the lies we tell ourselves throughout the day.

- **UNRAVELING ILLUSIONS**

In this chapter, we rummage into the complexities of self-deception and the art of embracing uncomfortable truths. Explore the intricacies of breaking free from ingrained patterns as we navigate the delicate balance between accepting criticism from loved ones and confronting the lies we tell ourselves. Through introspection, discover the empowering journey of dismantling illusions to foster genuine self-awareness and personal growth.

MIST AKES

"I believe that there is no such thing as mistakes. I've never missed a take; I've seized every opportunity given to me and taken full advantage of the lessons. I take in the losses as well!"

"God gave you a break to hear what He has for you to do. Rejoice and feel blessed that He has given you time instead of taking it."

Peace #GBC
~Larry Coleman

The Insight

THE INSIGHT

God is taking me through some things. It seems like the more I give and confess my heart's desires, the road of tests gets tougher, challenging my peace of mind from every angle. I've encountered spirits of giving up more often, trying to befriend me. I'm a very friendly person, but I really don't want to be cool with these cats at all. My definition of faith has changed, and I need to know the right definition now. Can somebody tell me what it means? I'm really asking for help. I have some serious soul-searching to do, and I need to be strong to overcome my demons. The beautiful thing in all this is that my "crazy-but-ain't-tired-of-fighting-no-more" attitude is strong. I plan on being here to make an impact on the world while I'm in this form.

At the age of 25, I found myself at a point in my life where I was troubled by how my world was turning. I felt a lot of heartbreak and loneliness. Trying to figure it all out, I was a young father of 2 by two different women and struggling with that old messed up term I hate with a passion (baby mama drama), my family was tripping, my sisters never really got along as sisters should, my finances were ok, but I was hemorrhaging money like crazy, and I was just sad! So one night, I had enough, and I did what any person going through a rough patch in life feels like they're at rock bottom. I fell on my knees, cried out to my God, begged for forgiveness, and asked and pleaded for God to send me a sign and deliver me, and all I want is to live in your will and have peace of Mind and Happiness. And then I was blessed with my Peace of Mind and Happiness. You, my Hana' Sahar. I love you, my prayer to God....

I know I tell you time And time again how much I love you and how proud I am to be your father , but words can't really describe the love and joy I feel when I look at you and hear your precious voice. You truly are my heartbeat above all. Love Dad

WHAT I LEARNED ABOUT FORGIVENESS

I learned how to forgive from my mother. She was a beautiful soul who lived her life according to God's words. One of her famous quotes was 'Feed them with a long handle spoon.' Initially, I thought it meant shoving a long stick down someone's throat if they wronged me, but she truly meant forgiving and showing kindness.

She forgave some of the most evil people and remained kind to them. I used to get mad hearing her cry, thinking someone had been mean to her. However, I later discovered she cried out to God in prayer to heal and bless those people, asking God to alleviate their pain. Her tears were not for herself but for them.

After my mother passed away, I moved in with my dad and asked him about her. He confirmed the positive things she had told me over the years. Having had her in my life made it easy to see my dad as the hero my mother described. She never spoke negatively about him, and he only repeated her words.

Embracing the Legacy

In the wake of my mother's passing, I found solace in the enduring lessons of forgiveness she imparted. Each day became a chapter in the book of healing, a testament to her unwavering faith and kindness.

As I navigated life under my father's roof, I discovered that the hero my mother spoke of was not just a narrative but a living embodiment. He echoed her words, reinforcing the importance of forgiveness and compassion. In my understanding deepened, and I began to weave the threads of her legacy into the fabric of my own existence.

The echoes of her famous phrase, "Feed them with a long handle spoon," resonated within me. I realized it wasn't about retaliation but extending grace even in the face of wrongdoing. The challenging moments became opportunities to emulate her strength, to forgive as she forgave.

Despite the distance, her presence lingered, guiding me through the complexities of life. I sought refuge in her teachings, understanding that true forgiveness transcends personal grievances. Her tears, once a mystery, now revealed a profound love that reached beyond herself—a love that prayed for the redemption and healing of even the most malevolent souls.

This memory unfolded with a realization that forgiveness, as my mother lived it, wasn't a passive act but a transformative force. I embraced her legacy not just as a memory but as a living principle, shaping my relationships and interactions. In honoring her memory, I discovered the power of forgiveness to heal wounds and mend the fractures within the human experience. As the pages turned, I carried forward the essence of her spirit, a beacon of light in my journey of understanding and embracing the true meaning of forgiveness.

Her lessons has shaped me into the person I am today always wanting love and peace for everyone . knowing that kindness is always the easiest fix for every problem, and it is the easiest thing in the world to do. I pray that my family of brothers sisters, nieces, nephews, aunts, uncles, sons, daughters, husbands, wives, grandchildren, cousins, and friends all recall to memory, the love that God has made in order for us to learn what forgiveness means.

IF I DID

"If I did" is not an apology. Learn to forgive and forget, and stop leaving it alone. We often think we're being forgiving when we offer a so-called apology despite knowing we don't believe we're wrong. We give a weak, meaningless apology like, "If I did something to hurt you or if you feel like I said something wrong, I'm asking you to forgive me!" It is condescending and rude. Instead, be sincere in your plea for peace and resolution. Say, "I sincerely apologize for making you feel that way." I had no idea, and that was never my intention. Would you please accept my apology?"

Regarding "an eye for an eye," it signifies reciprocity, not revenge. It's the duality of life—good and evil, action and reaction, cause and effect. Embrace the willingness to listen, learn, and stop the cycle.

On visiting grave sites, I don't because I believe I've laid my loved ones to rest in my mind. Grave sites are for the dead, symbolizing burying not only physical remains but also dead mentalities and issues like bitterness, unforgiveness, and negativity. Conversations repeatedly revisiting past grievances don't interest me; my response is, "I don't visit grave sites."

My notes are titled "Let Me Set This Right Here."

"Reckoning and Release"
It becomes evident that the phrase "If I did" falls short of genuine remorse. True forgiveness requires acknowledging the wrongdoing without hesitation and the importance of sincerity in seeking peace and resolution.

The concept of "an eye for an eye" is dissected beyond the surface of revenge. It represents life's inherent duality—where good and evil, action and reaction, coexist. Understanding this equilibrium is crucial for breaking the cycle and fostering genuine connections.

Our journey is introspective as we discuss the choice not to visit grave sites. This personal decision is rooted in the belief that laying loved ones to rest in the mind transcends the physical act.

The chapter concludes with a reflection on the title of our notes, "Let Me Set This Right Here," emphasizing the significance of addressing and resolving matters with intention and care. As we navigate through apologies, reciprocity, and personal choices, the essence lies in setting things right, allowing for reckoning, and ultimately finding a path to release.

MY APOLOGY

"Good morning. How are you doing? I want to start by expressing my love for you and praying that you love yourself and God as well. It has weighed heavily on my heart, and now God is working on me in ways I never knew. Let me begin by releasing all the demons that have plagued my life and my loved ones. I will stand against the devil and fight for our freedom. I rebuke all of Satan's plans and past deeds that have come against me and my people. I ask for your forgiveness for all the pain I have caused in your life. I also ask you to forgive yourselves for any pain you may have caused in your own lives. I pray that you will forgive me for any ill feelings, words, or actions I may have been a part of that caused harm to your mind and your ability to thrive and be happy in this life. I am truly ashamed and show humble remorse for my role in causing pain in our lives.

I have been praying and asking God to heal my heart and mind, to cleanse my soul, and to purify my heart so that I and my people may enjoy the prosperity that God has prepared for us in this life. I say to you now, forgive yourself and others because what happened to you as a child has been judged and forgiven by God. It can no longer hurt you; it was not our fault. What we did as adults to cause pain and hurt has been judged and forgiven by God.

So, today, let's mark a new day and agree not to let the past pain, hurt, and unforgiving spirits live beyond tomorrow. Today, I ask you to agree to make the same plea to all those you have had ill feelings toward—seek forgiveness and forgive them. If you do not have the courage or the words, give them this message.

I have been in counsel, and I am no longer embarrassed by the past, nor am I ashamed anymore because the Devil is a lie. God is my King and the Guide over my life, and I cannot be moved. So, I say, take advantage, join in on the opportunity to clean up and reward your life with the blessings of peace and happiness. I love you all, and I pray you love me back and love yourself the same."

Peace,
Mr. Larry Coleman

BETTER THAN ME

Man, I can't stand it when people say, "You think you're better than me!" People don't like the fact that you are better at being you than they are at being themselves. So, they say, "You think you're better than me." I'm just better at being me than you are at being you!
"Befriend an ENEMY"
- Larry Coleman

UNIT THREE

VISION

"While I understand that my visions may not be your dream, I pray that just maybe my vision can serve as fuel and clarity for your dreams!"
-Larry Coleman

Vision

PERCEPTION

Being an entrepreneur is tough, especially without money or support for your goals. However, that is self-deception because when you're the boss of your own life, you must create everything. I grew up in a small town where good opportunities were very limited, where young men were always tempted to choose illegal paths that lead to false success. Like most of them, I dabbled and made mistakes, but I refocused and decided that I wanted more out of life.

One of my most important lessons from my past is that you have the power to create and adjust the rules as often as you need to. There are no rules hindering you when it's your journey. Never lose confidence in yourself or your dreams; trust yourself always. You can lie to others, but never to yourself. The only time you're allowed to lie to yourself is to create something out of nothing, like when I was growing up in Hugo after my mom's death. I refused to believe she was gone until I was 17, needing to believe my life was good and I had a reason to live. I aspired to be rich and successful, imagining doing wonderful things for my mom.

Although it wasn't my reality then, it became one as everything I told myself began happening. Now at a crossroads, life in return for its favors has beaten me up. I'm challenged to recreate and find the mental energy to bring visions to life. Being a big liar to yourself is necessary; tell your mind, body, and soul that you have the energy to believe again. It's the crazy essence of being the leader of your own destiny — "investing in your perception until it becomes your reality".- Larry Coleman

SOCIAL STATUS

Note to self when you see me celebrate my achievements on social media or otherwise, please don't think that's an opportunity to ask me for money!

I was told by someone that they never see any pictures of me doing any charity work like giving out turkey dinners etc.. my response was "Oh, I'm sorry my giving is not social media friendly. It is so much and so fast and so often it's kind of hard to capture it on camera...

Matthew 6:1-4

My life was looking pretty bad until I changed my lenses!

Larry Coleman

MY VIEW

Some people only want to showcase the beautiful aspects on the path to success. Well, I'm here to tell you that's a lie because the road to success is filled with failures, ups and downs. If someone only shows you the positives, they may not be truly honest about the journey. There might be a selfish agenda behind it; they haven't found the true path. I'm going to show you the whole picture.

As an artist, when I was painting and composing music, some of my best work started as complete chaos. The beauty of creating art is that the picture doesn't always start well; sometimes, life's best moments come with a murky beginning. My life hasn't always been great, even at the top of my financial ladder. My view was marred by heartache, confusion, jealousy, and depression.

It was when I was dead broke that I discovered I was truly rich and most pleased with myself. The art of true wealth is maintaining peace and happiness while achieving. When things seem bad, understand that it might not be bad at all; perhaps, it's just the focus you have on it. The simple fix to bad focus is to change your lens.

The Boss

THE BOSS

"I didn't realize I was filthy rich until I was dead broke. It was then that I truly grasped the power of giving. Despite facing one of the lowest points in my life, unsure of where to turn, and lacking clarity about turning to God, I felt compelled to do so. Although I didn't fully understand what turning to God meant, even in my ignorance, I believe the Most High provided me with clarity. I saw giving as a way out of the pit I was in. It was at this moment that I felt my spirit lift, and enlightenment came to me through the act of giving, even when I had no money to my name. With a pure mind and heartfelt intent, the more I gave, the more abundantly I could give, as if I were a wealthy man. That's when it dawned on me that I was truly rich because I understood what it meant to be wealthy in the Lord. I didn't realize I was filthy rich until I was dead broke."

– Larry Coleman

SPITE

"We say I made it in spite of all the nay-saying, but be careful, cause sometimes we might just be living and making it in spite!" - Larry Coleman

THE LITTLE THINGS

"If you think you are too small to do big things,
then do small things in a big way!"
– Larry Coleman

LET'S TALK ABOUT IT

THINKING RICH

(Health and Wealth Rhyme for a Reason)

Thinking rich is exactly what it is. You should structure your thoughts like a Fortune 500 company, but first, you must understand how a successful business operates from top to bottom, then realize that you are the company!

I like to compare my understanding to health and relationships: my relationships with my employees, insurance agent, realtor, doctors, accountants, bankers, chef, dietitian, housekeeping, and all those that help me put together my way of Thinking Rich.

To stay healthy and lucrative, we need all functional parties in place. My realtor will help keep my properties (house) in order! By securing properties to operate my several businesses, I keep all my accounts straight so I can afford to keep my company afloat. That's where my insurance agent comes into play to ensure all my relationships are safeguarded with the right coverage, so that my assets are protected at all times, and my banker will keep me in check so I can finance my operations just in case. I need to visit my doctor who will keep me informed on how my body is operating. I need to be healthy for the internal and external to run right, so I don't have strangers around me.

Just as I maintain a working relationship with my doctor and the specialists overseeing my health, I apply the same principle to those involved in the management of my wealth. I have the best staff to clean house, especially when things get dirty. My chef provides the best healthy meals to make sure I am in the best health I can be. He works together with my dietitian, my doctor, my insurance agent, and my personal trainer. they all follow my orders.

I took control of health by learning everything I could about myself and my body . I think and speak rich in every way possible . That means when I encounter negativity I try my best to see things in a positive light. Once you've learned to create a mindset of thinking in a positive rich manner your life will become clear in a way that transcends the normal understanding of life and how you respond to it. Think Rich and watch your overall Health and Wealth increase.

Lastly, consider this thought! Its been said that, "broke men don't golf" so if your broke, golf isn't for you! But I'd like to say that a broke MINDSET doesn't golf. Simply put, you have to have your shit together!

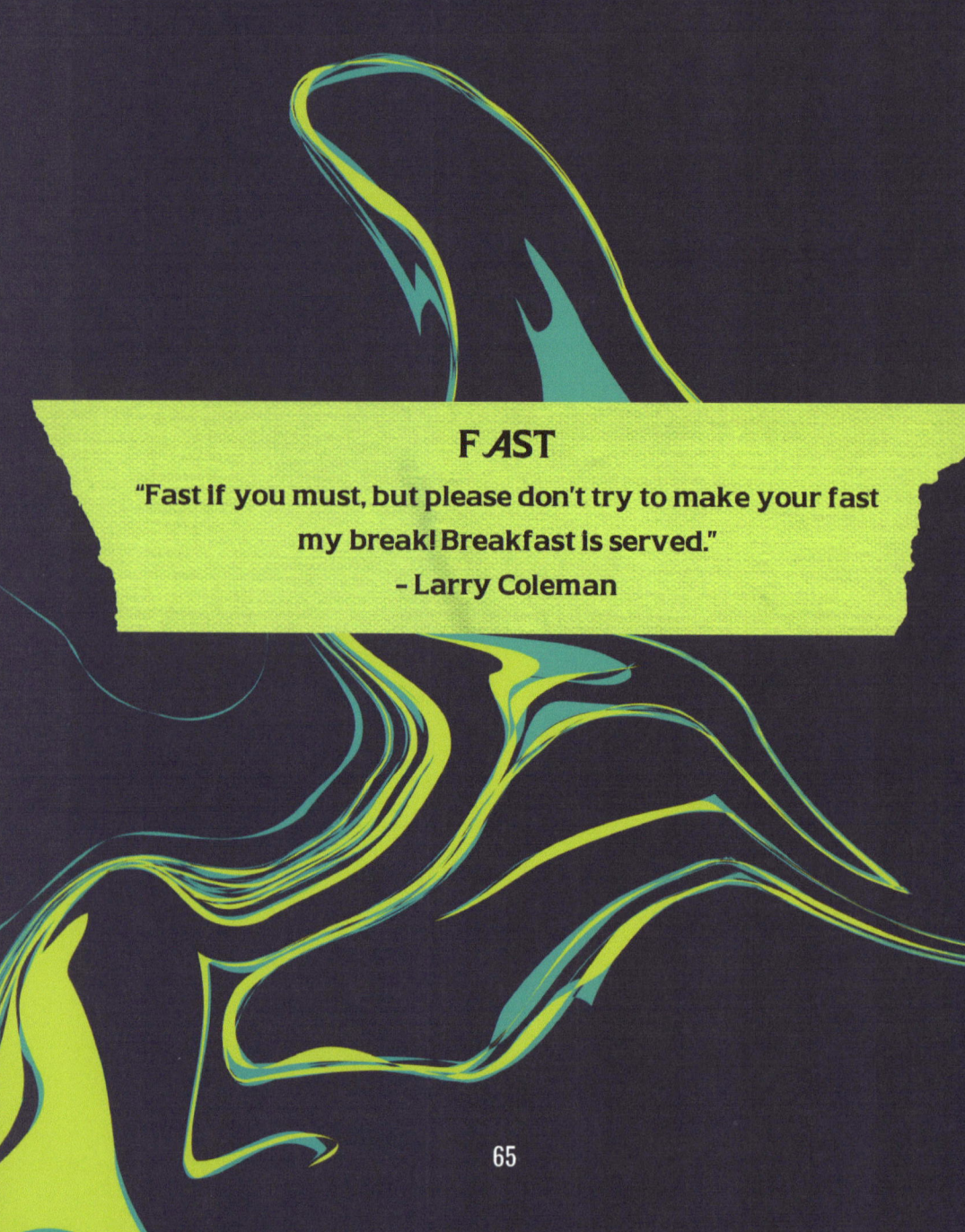

FAST

"Fast if you must, but please don't try to make your fast my break! Breakfast is served."
– Larry Coleman

DO SOMETHING

"Do something when you are in the moment of doing something different. Do something different!"
– Larry Coleman

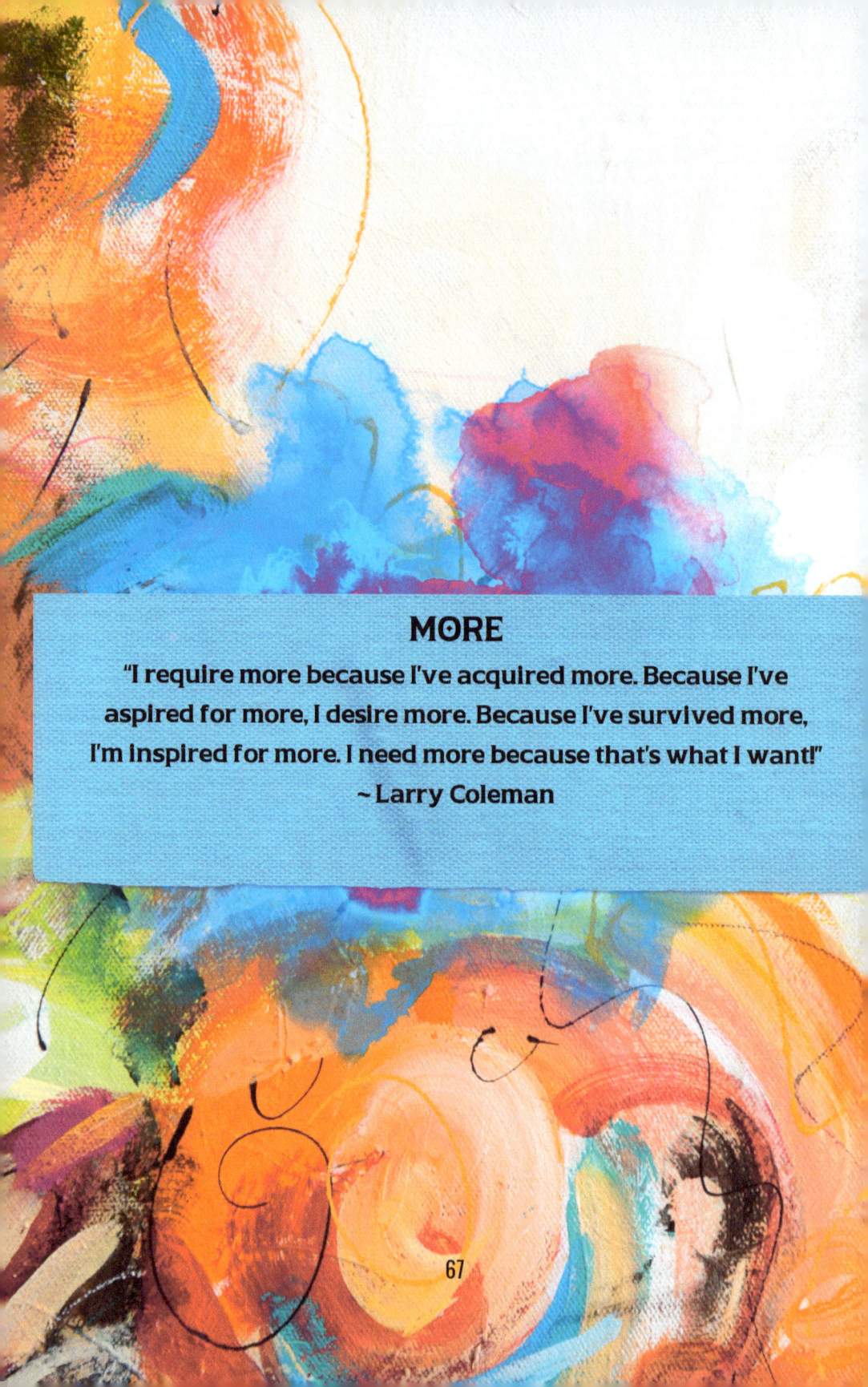

MORE

"I require more because I've acquired more. Because I've aspired for more, I desire more. Because I've survived more, I'm inspired for more. I need more because that's what I want!"
~ Larry Coleman

THE KEY TO SUCCESS

The key to success is mastering time, ensuring you're not too busy to handle your business. Get busy on not being busy; make sure you own your time. Nothing is more valuable than owning your time, so delegate it in proper priority fashion. I like to implement a percentage value system into my lifestyle, for example: 100% cannot be given to anything, as someone or something loses out on value and time. Life priorities are God first, then family, and so on. The question is, how do you divide your time among things or people you care about? The mastery of this will determine when you become a true success story. So, brush up on your math, as life math is far more complex than simple numbers can begin to express. Know your mathematics; add it up to see how it divides all of us.

Time Mastery and Success Equation
In the pursuit of success we investigate the crucial concept of mastering time as the linchpin for achieving your goals. Here, we explore practical strategies to navigate the delicate balance between busyness and productivity.

Unraveling the Time Paradox
In this section, we unravel the paradox of time—how being too busy can hinder rather than propel success. By emphasizing the importance of managing your schedule effectively, we shed light on the need to prioritize tasks and responsibilities.

Owning Your Time
Emphasizes the significance of ownership when it comes to time. Readers are guided on the journey to reclaiming control over their schedules and lives. Practical tips and actionable advice are presented to empower individuals to assertively own their time.

The Value of Delegation
This section digs into the art of delegation, illustrating the power of wisely allocating time to different priorities. The narrative unfolds with anecdotes and insights into how successful individuals leverage delegation to enhance their efficiency.

The Percentage Value System
introduces the percentage value system as a lifestyle tool. Readers are encouraged to assign values to different aspects of their lives, ensuring a balanced distribution of time. Real-life examples and case studies illustrate the transformative impact of this approach.

Life's Equation
Concludes with an exploration of life's equation. Readers are prompted to reflect on the fundamental question: How do you divide your time among the things and people you care about? This introspective journey sets the stage for the mastery that determines one's trajectory towards becoming a true success story.

Closing Thoughts: Navigating Life's Complex Math
In the closing remarks, the chapter emphasizes the intricate nature of life's mathematical equation. Readers are encouraged to understand and embrace the complexity, recognizing that success is not merely about simple numbers but a nuanced and strategic allocation of time and energy. I need you to remember this, learn your percentages not knowing your integers could injure a relationship so get back to the basics quick. Geometry is an anomaly to the economy ,caught up by distractions, making up small fractions, thru fashion our passions blind us from seeing the math not matching these subtractions keep distracting us from adding love to the equation of us!

This serves as a pivotal guide, urging readers to sharpen their time-management skills and encouraging them to embark on a journey of self-discovery in the pursuit of a successful and fulfilling life.

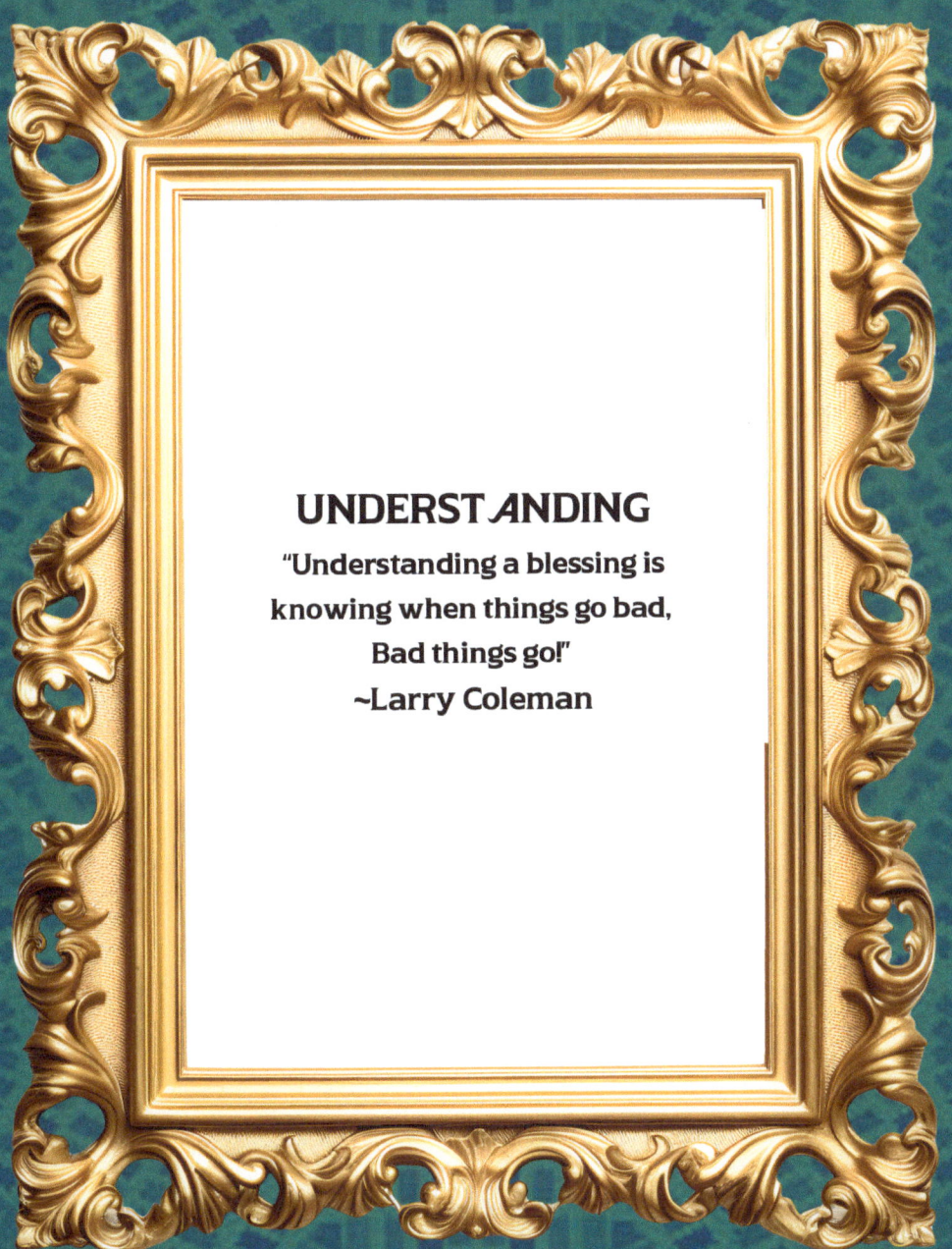

UNDERSTANDING

"Understanding a blessing is knowing when things go bad, Bad things go!"
~Larry Coleman

UNIT FOUR

LOSS

"Loss" What I've learned about loss is quite different from how people may perceive it. I see loss as God's way of replenishing His energy, essentially recycling His creations. It has been said that when someone dies, another is born. Therefore, I believe that with every loss, a new product emerges. While we, as humans, often mourn our losses to varying degrees, I've come to understand and mourn the loss in my way as I've grown. The more attached we are to possessions or loved ones, the harder it is to let go. As a child, my mother instilled in us the value of sharing our possessions, teaching us to give to those who might need or appreciate them more. Although I initially resisted, reflecting on those lessons made me realize that we often fail to understand the value of our possessions until it's time to part with them. This insight taught me not to be selfish and to appreciate even the most minor things. I am grateful to my mother for building character and preparing me for the losses I've faced and those yet to come. I now understand loss as a cleansing process, a way to create harmony where there was once chaos. While mourning is a natural response if we are honest with ourselves, we might choose relief every time – God's way of recycling His creations, including our possessions.

A Shift in Perspective
In the tapestry of life, the threads of loss weave a pattern that often eludes our understanding. My perception of loss has evolved into a unique lens through which I view the ebb and flow of existence. It's a perspective distinct from the conventional narrative surrounding loss, one that sees it as a cosmic act of rejuvenation orchestrated by a higher power.

I contemplate loss as God's subtle method of replenishing divine energy, an intricate process of recycling creations. Embedded in this philosophy is the notion that when one life departs, another is summoned into being. This cyclical dance between departure and arrival, mourning and celebration, shapes the intricate balance of the universe.

As humans, we navigate the currents of grief, each mourning our losses in a manner as individual as the fingerprints that mark our identity. Yet, a common thread binds us — the recognition that loss is an inevitable companion on our journey. In my maturation, I've come to apprehend loss in a way that transcends the ordinary, a realization that the possessions we cling to may exist more in our minds than in the tangible world.

The paradox unfolds: the more fervently we grasp our possessions or cherish our loved ones, the more arduous it becomes to release them. It's a lesson etched in the fabric of my childhood, where my mother imparted the wisdom of sharing and selflessness. Initially resistant, I learned that the true essence of possessions lies not in their physical form but in the value we place upon them.

My mother's teachings guided me to appreciate the most minor things and discern the value in the tiniest possessions. Gratitude, I discovered, is a powerful antidote to the sting of loss. I owe a debt of gratitude to my mother, for she sculpted my character and equipped me to face life's inevitable losses.

As I navigate the labyrinth of existence, I've come to regard loss not merely as a source of sorrow but as a catalyst for growth. It serves as a mirror reflecting the impermanence of our attachments, urging us to release our burdens. Perhaps loss is God's way of initiating a cosmic reset, a cleansing of souls to restore harmony where chaos once reigned.

In the chapters that follow, I will delve deeper into the nuances of loss, exploring its multifaceted nature and the transformative power it holds. For now, consider this the prologue to a journey of understanding, acceptance, and profound wisdom concealed within the folds of loss.

RULE 2737

In the realm of Rule 2737, life spans approximately a million days. It all began with a battle among millions of sperm cells, and you emerged as the chosen one to live. This singular privilege is the foundation for the million reasons you should seek to sustain your existence. However, if, despite this multitude of reasons, you ever find yourself with no alternative, then and only then can death be considered an option.

I define a reason as either an excuse or an option to avoid the struggles of life. In this journey, you have no other choice but to select life. How you choose to live is entirely your decision. Nonetheless, ponder this: if you opt for life, you don't require a reason to survive; you endure and strive each day. When adversity strikes, the temptation may arise to search for a reason to surrender. But remember, you must navigate through a million reasons before concluding that you have exhausted your choices for living.

(Deuteronomy 30:19)

DEPRESSION

"Depression arises when you spend too much time pondering what happened to you instead of making things happen for you".
~ Larry Coleman

DEPRESSION

We will experience two deaths: a spiritual death and a natural one. There are two types of depression—clinical and the one I want to discuss with you today."

Self-induced Depression: Say it with me it happened, and it is not happening now!

I'm sorry; I have a terrible memory, and I forgot I was supposed to be mad at you for something that happened a long time ago. I know you said I hurt you when we were kids, and you just had to tell me about myself regarding that issue. Honestly, you were probably dealing with Superman, Batman, or some other superhero I was trying to be then. My bad!

Plus, let me slow down so I can cut your pant leg loose from my bumper. I didn't realize you got caught up on my bumper, and I've been dragging you all this time. I surely don't want to cause more harm, so let me pull over to the side and cut you loose so that you don't roll into oncoming traffic and get run over again by someone else. I do apologize, though!

ABUSE

(Abuse)
(A + B) = USE

YOU + ME = US = (E)

    1.   environment
    2.   exercise
    3.   emotions

(Abuse, depression, addiction) = parenting
Repetition = addiction

(Abuse) X - y (weed, alcohol, drugs) = a, b (Factor). (Habit)

"Tolerate it so you can articulate it."

The number one offense we commit as parents when it comes to sin is disobeying one important commandment by Christ: "Care for the little ones." The little things are the children to me. The children, the little things we neglect, children in the company of adults; we don't listen to them (the children) when they try to tell us what is going on! We shut them down; we shut them up in a room with other children when we have adult company. We scold them for talking to us in front of adults. We don't consider the fact that they might be getting molested right under our nose.

I decided to create my own equation to figure out my own addictions, my repetitions, and find a cure to fix the reason I keep my repetitions going. We all have our own vices, but I really want to solve the problem. We all share in this world, and I believe the answer is in the math. The universal truth, simple math, is the universal truth. It surpasses all things like race, religion, sex, social status, and everything else.

If we look at the simple math, we will learn to agree with things like love and caring for the most important people in the world: The children. The reason I say the children are that they are the future and the present state of world affairs. What I mean by this is simple; the way we care for our children will determine how they will be when they become adults, and in my opinion, we have done a horrible job.

Now let's go back to the math equation. It is the children and the most children that grow up dealing with mental, drug, and sex issues and other types of abuse, depression (some common, some I preface for the sake of respecting all people and their preferences, but I say some homosexuality) when asked a group of 50 people; all said the same thing: their first introduction to abuse came when they were very young children. And they still like that till this day all behind their abuse and their addiction, such as sex, drugs, mental issues, and etc.

So with that being said, I've termed children and abuse the same thing—the little things. We have a problem ignoring the little things, and those little things are: don't interrupt grown folks while they're talking, go in your room and play with your cousin while grown folks are partying. Meanwhile, most abuse has happened when children are closed up in rooms with older cousins, siblings, and friends without adult supervision. As we ignore the little things when they try to talk to us in the middle of an adult conversation, shaking my head. The sad part is, maybe the little thing was trying to tell you that while you were partying and drinking in the front room with your friends, one of those drunk adults came into the room on the way to the bathroom and molested them while you were busy, kicking it with your bad parenting—a repetitive style we all fall short with, but it has become the leading cause of the majority of today's abuse. I believe that's why one of those things said by Jesus was, "Care for the little things, do not hinder them." If you are a follower, you should know what it commands in the Gospel, so I say we have not done our part to care for the little things.

I-35 and Dying

I-35 AND DYING

I know this might sound crazy, but truth is. I've spent so much time traveling up and down I-35 since my babies lived in Texas, and I resided in OKC. Many times, I faced life and death situations on my trips to and from Texas. Each call from my babies or their mothers prompted me to hit the road, sometimes speeding like a bat out of hell. Rain, sleet, snow, and even tornadoes couldn't deter me; I was dedicated to being a great dad.

It was always heartwarming when my baby girl would call, expressing her desire to see me or asking me to pick her up from school. I'd respond with an enthusiastic "Sure, I'm on my way!" I'd roll out in the middle of the night, no matter the weather, because being there for my kids made my day.

Despite these joyful moments, I couldn't shake the feeling that I-35 was a dying drive. In 2008, as the last few years passed filled with heartache and pain, my drives along I-35 turned into revelations of haunting pain and past mistakes.

As time passed, I found myself navigating I-35 while grappling with depression and grief. Nights in the ICU room, witnessing my daughter's suffering, led me to pray for a way to alleviate her pain. I'd willingly take on all her illness to grant her a normal, healthy life. One day, while driving home on I-35, lost in thoughts of my baby and past losses, the rain poured down hard. I found myself between two diesel trucks, contemplating giving in to despair. I let the wheel go, expecting the car to swerve and crash, but it stayed straight, almost as if someone intervened. That moment made me realize that God had a different plan for me, a promise to keep.

I've had several nervous breakdowns on I-35. One instance in a Dallas hotel room, reminiscent of times with my daughter, brought uncontrollable crying and shaking spells. The realization hit me that she was no longer here. My wife, thankfully coincidentally in Dallas, had to drive me back home, reminding me of my promise and the importance of not giving up.

During another breakdown on I-35, my wife's support helped me regain focus. Despite the challenges, I began working on the promise I made to my daughter after my experience with I-35 and Dying.

ICU

I can remember when we first learned that Taletha had lupus, which, at the time, was diagnosed as discoid lupus affecting the skin. She had a rash on her back that my wife noticed, so we contacted her mom, and we all agreed to get it looked at by a doctor. That's how it all began - lupus! "What the hell!" It seemed like as soon as we took in the news, she was three weeks in the ICU. I was mind-blown.

I remember it clear as day. I was at the shop in the middle of a cut when the phone rang. Her mom, as calm as she could be at the time, said, "When can you get to Dallas? Your baby is in the ICU, and they say it doesn't look good." I was like, "What?" I had just spoken with my baby earlier that day, confirming she got the money I had sent her. So, I had to finish with my client, then walk outside to catch my breath and prepare to make a three-hour drive to Texas to see my daughter in the ICU.

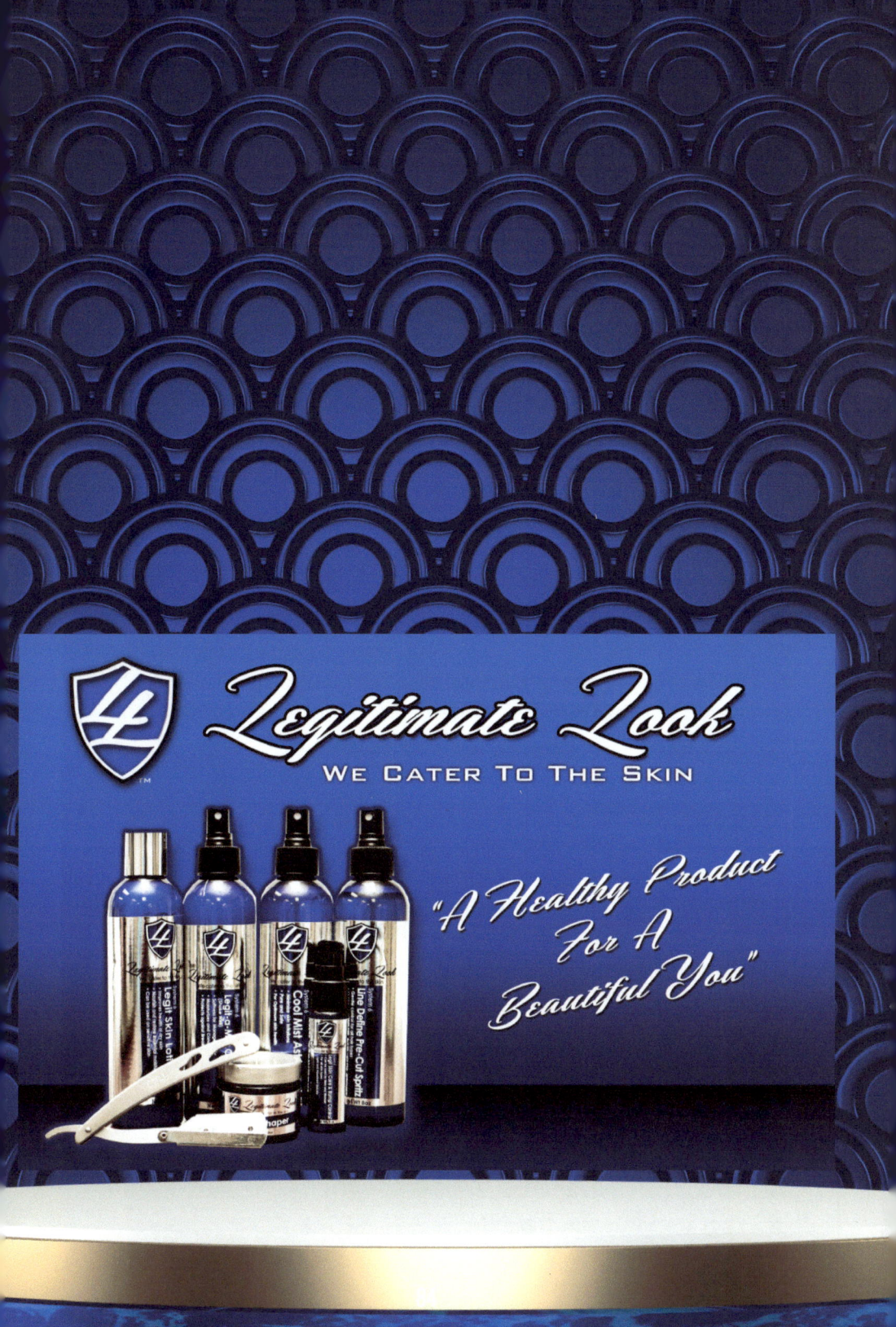

ACCEPTANCE
(For her condition and mine)

We need to decide whether we'll succumb to this disease or choose to fight and lead a fulfilling life despite the challenges she faces every moment.

The birth of the Legitimate Look product evolved because we tried everything to aid our battle with Lupus. I remember the rashes and sunlight sensitivity issues we confronted. Late at night, I prayed for a formula to alleviate some of the pain my baby endured after countless days, weeks, and hours of research and development.

I devised a system to care for my baby through diet, exercise, and meditation. We created System 6, which not only improved her outward appearance but also alleviated internal pain. She accepted her fate but didn't want others to suffer, believing in System 6 and urging me to help others with it.

A Promise to Share
As the Legitimate Look product gained momentum, Acceptance unfolded with a promise to share our hard-fought journey battling Lupus. It was a chapter born out of resilience, filled with the echoes of countless nights spent researching and developing a formula to ease the pain my baby faced.

the focus shifted to the creation of System 6, a comprehensive approach encompassing diet, exercise, and meditation. The narrative delved into the transformative impact of System 6 on both outward appearance and internal well-being. It became the cornerstone of acceptance for my baby, who, having faced numerous pain-staking days, weeks, and hours, found solace in the fact that this was her fate.

But acceptance did not translate to resignation. Instead, it fueled a commitment to prevent others from enduring similar suffering. System 6 chronicled the genesis of a promise—made by my baby—to share System 6 with the world. It became a beacon of hope for those grappling with Lupus, a testament to the belief that a good life could be lived despite the challenges posed by the relentless disease. In the unfolding chapters of our journey, the promise made would resonate, as Legitimate Look became more than a product—it became a symbol of resilience, shared with the world in the spirit of compassion and understanding.

"My Almond Eyes"
Taletha Coleman
1991–2013

GETTING OFF-ENDED

Getting off-ended instead of getting offended, we stay on the road to success and happiness. Occasionally, boredom or distraction sets in due to the extended journey. When we spot an off-ramp, the allure is strong, tempting us to explore attractions waiting on the off-ended path. It's easy to get off-ended when our focus shifts from the road."

Navigating the Off-Ramps
In the journey toward success and happiness, we encounter the inevitable off-ramps that can divert us from our intended path. These detours often arise when monotony or distraction sets in after a prolonged period of travel on the road to our goals.

As we've ventured along the right road, the allure of an off-ramp becomes tempting. The attractions waiting at the off-end of our road entice us, prompting a desire to explore new avenues. However, yielding to this temptation can lead to a state of being "off-ended."

Explore the challenges of maintaining focus and resilience when faced with off-ramps. It delves into the importance of recognizing these distractions, understanding their allure, and developing strategies to stay steadfast on the road to success.

Hitting Home

HITTING HOME

Bravery is a term often used but seldom practiced. My little Almond Eyes personified this concept. One day, after a prolonged stint in the ICU, she called me. She asked me to confront the reality that she was unwell and that one day she would pass away. Although it was heart-wrenching, our four-hour conversation revealed that my first-born was preparing me for life after her.

She sent me pictures of her face, urging me to look beyond the swelling and blisters, to see the beauty she saw. She wanted me to understand that true beauty and love endure, even as outward appearances fade. I always saw my child as a beautiful queen, but she wanted me to see beyond the pain, preparing me for a future I couldn't fathom at the time. In those moments, God used my daughter to reveal his glory and beauty through the innocence of a child. I had to look through and past the suffering to comprehend that blessings follow pain. Despite my intense suffering, I heeded my daughter's plea as a father who yearned to give his child the world. I listened closely, and when the time came, I was astounded.

For a while, I lived on autopilot until the memory of my promise to her brought me back. Then, like a ton of bricks, it hit me—I want to live; I have to live. I have a promise to fulfill and a duty as a father, a mission granted by God.

AND A CHILD SHALL LEAD

My daughter, Taletha, was one of the most brutally honest people I ever met. Even when she lied, she told me the truth. I'll get to that later on! She covered for her mom so much that it broke my heart but made me respect her so much and understand what real love and compassion meant. Before she got really ill, she would always ask me to be honest at all times. She would say, "Daddy, don't ever lie to me. I can handle whatever it is," and she was like 9 years old, saying stuff like this. My baby was super bold and kind at the same time. What impressed me the most is she never liked her parents or anyone fighting with each other. She made me promise to always tell the truth, no matter what, even if it hurt someone's feelings. She said never give in to a lie to keep the peace with anyone. She told me to never cheat or steal, to always be kind at all times to anyone, and to love with all my heart. She made me promise this!

Echoes of Promise

As the seasons changed, so did the rhythm of our lives. Taletha's wisdom echoed in my heart, a guiding light through the twists and turns of each passing day. In the quiet moments, her words resonated, reminding me of the promises we made.

The air was heavy with memories as I navigated the challenges of a world without her physical presence. Taletha's lessons fueled my determination to live by the principles she held dear. The honesty she championed became a beacon, illuminating the path through the shadows of grief.

In this chapter of life, I found solace in honoring her plea for truth. The echoes of her boldness and kindness inspired me to be a source of unwavering compassion. Taletha's insistence on avoiding lies to maintain peace lingered, urging me to navigate conflicts with sincerity.

As I tread through the pages of this chapter, I carried the weight of promises made. Never cheating or stealing, always extending kindness, and loving with all my heart became more than vows—they became the essence of my existence. Taletha's spirit, forever 9 years old, continued to guide, a poignant reminder that even a child could lead with enduring impact.

I PRAY YOU NEVER KNOW

I say this because when people mention they can't imagine losing a child, I wish that pain upon no one. Though I'm not the author of the day, I advocate for those who haven't felt such loss. So, I pray you never know. If you should ever imagine it, test your faith. God had to imagine losing His children when creating it all, so who are we not to? Just saying! "GBG."

We All Have to Cry

WE ALL HAVE TO CRY

It's like a scheduled appointment with God – a set time that you don't need to worry about missing or remembering because He has assistants (angels) to remind you of your upcoming appointment. Trust me, we all have several cries scheduled, so go ahead and have your cry. Ecclesiastes 3:1-8 says there is a time for everything, so go ahead have your cry it's okay.

JOY COMES IN THE MOURNING

We often get so offended by people and caught up in mourning that we can't see the joy on its way. Imagine having to bury your father on Friday and getting a call for a haircut appointment on Thursday while you are figuring out how to bury your father. But you need the money you'll make for the service on Thursday. What are you going to do? See the joy in your mourning or get caught up, missing a blessing God sent your way to receive it with the skill He gave you. IJS. Psalms 30:5 says, 'For his anger endures but a moment; in his favor is life: weeping may endure for a night, but joy comes in the morning.

In the quiet moments before the sunrise, where darkness and light engage in a delicate dance, we find ourselves at the threshold of hope. Life's journey often confronts us with unexpected challenges, akin to the burial of a loved one or the pressing need for provision in the face of sorrow.
Yet, as the sun graces the sky on that Thursday morning, a juxtaposition of grief and opportunity unfolds. Consider preparing to bid farewell to a father on Friday, only to receive a call for a haircut appointment on Thursday. The urgency of financial need intertwines with the impending farewell, forcing a choice upon us.

It is in these intricate moments that the essence of joy reveals itself. The delicate balance between mourning and anticipation, hardship and unexpected blessings, challenges us to perceive beyond the immediate sorrow. What if, in our mourning, a divine appointment awaits? A chance to utilize the skills bestowed upon us to not only sustain ourselves but to receive a blessing sent by a higher power.

Psalms 30:5 echoes through the chapters of our lives, reminding us that God's anger endures but a moment, and in His favor lies life. The night may be laden with tears, but as the morning unfolds, joy emerges.

In contemplating our journey, let us heed the wisdom encapsulated in the verse, recognizing that joy is not merely an abstract concept but a tangible force that greets us at the dawn of each new day.

As we navigate the complexities of human emotions, let us also consider the profound advice: "Make your anger so expensive that no one can afford it and your kindness so cheap that almost anyone can have it for free." In doing so, we craft a path adorned with grace, where the cost of anger pales before the richness of compassion is freely given.

May this chapter inspire you to embrace the dawn, recognize the interplay of joy and mourning, and navigate life's intricacies with resilience and gratitude.

Every word has a root; we love to say I'm setting boundaries. I keep my circles small, but be careful because 'bound' is also a part of the word 'boundaries.' We put up big fences and enclose ourselves in small prisons, trying to isolate ourselves instead of creating a safe space.

"Be a little careful and learn what words mean so we can define our lives a little better."
~Larry Coleman

P.S. (Post Script)

I tried to name everyone in my prayer because that's how my mother would pray. She would name everybody she could think of when asking God to bless someone, so I'm trying to follow up with my memory, and I'm reminded every day because my wife prays the same way!

Lol, I joke with her about her long prayers, but honestly, it's refreshing because it brings back a memory of my mother every day!

VOCABULARY WORDS

Mental retardation: is not a normal definition as of the rest of society I believe retardation is mentally stagnant in your development. It goes for the comprehension, vocabulary, communication, etc. when you struggle to comprehend it's hard to communicate your emotions you become bitter, messy and unforgiving you keep a lot of mess going that is mental retardation.

Depression: is sitting around thinking about what happened to you instead of making something happen for you. Depression is like an addiction- repeating past abuses, offenses, attractions, then replacing that addition with the thought of abuse by adding a booster to give that thought energy disguised as drugs, excuses, liquor, sex, gambling etc.

GBG: Guided By God.

Practicing Addiction and Depression: is fixing your favorite snack and drink of your choice getting real cozy on the on the sofa with your favorite remote and tuning into your favorite movie starring you watching the same scene over and over again especially the sad scenes. Note to self change the channel it's easy to watch another movie maybe a superhero movie that you are starring in as the hero not the victim.

The baby: the child mindset, that's neglected, the new neglected person inside the innocent part of you, the guardian of your soul .

Mistake: an opportunity not taken or moved on or missed.

Abuse: the neglect of children harming little ones, the repetition of environmental influences that condone the violence, the violation of the rule to protect and respect, and to never harm children, the mathematical equation of depression, addiction, and violence.

Addiction: the definition of addiction, abuse, and depression is essentially repetition! Now, let's delve into understanding the mathematics and solving the equation. Let's identify the factors and demonstrate our process. I acknowledge this may diverge from conventional logic, but that's precisely the essence—I don't adhere to traditional theories. I had the audacity to redefine my life and the terminology that resonates with my experiences and their significance.

About the Author

Larry Coleman

Meet the author, a proud native of the small town of Hugo, shaped by its tight-knit community and the embrace of a big family. Fueled by a passion for storytelling, I draw inspiration from the colorful experiences of my roots. As a barbershop CEO, I navigate the artistry of grooming with a purpose. Beyond the clippers, I'm an artist in various realms, a devoted husband, a dad sculpting memories, and an enthusiast who finds solace in the green expanse of the golf course. This is my tale - a fusion of family, entrepreneurship, art, and the simple joys of life.

https://www.legithousepublishing.com/

Legitimatelook1@gmail.com
Facebook: @LarryColeman
Instagram: Legitdabarber

www.ingramcontent.com/pod-product-compliance
Lightning Source LLC
Chambersburg PA
CBHW041626220426
4366JCB00001B/26